I0413880

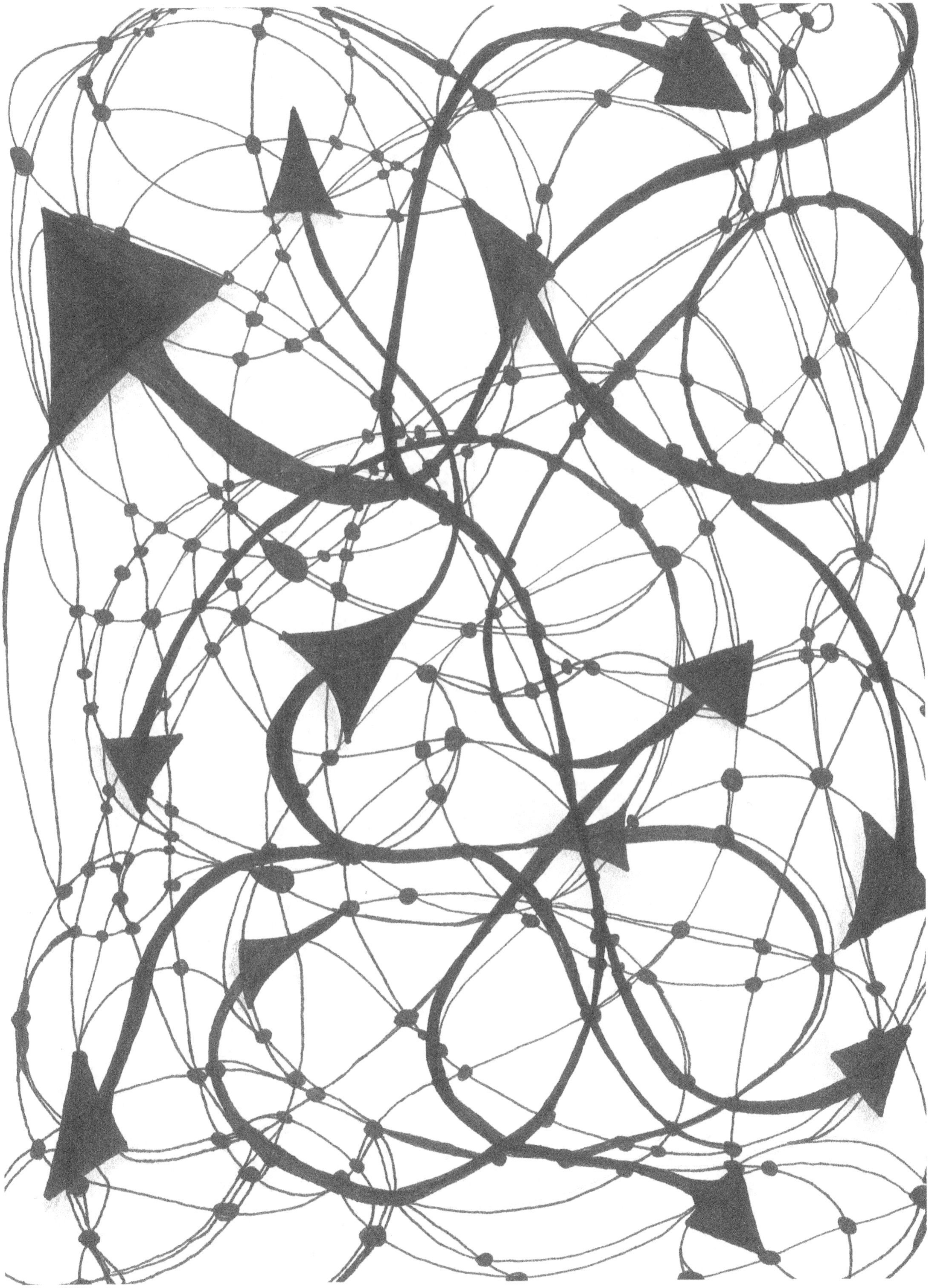

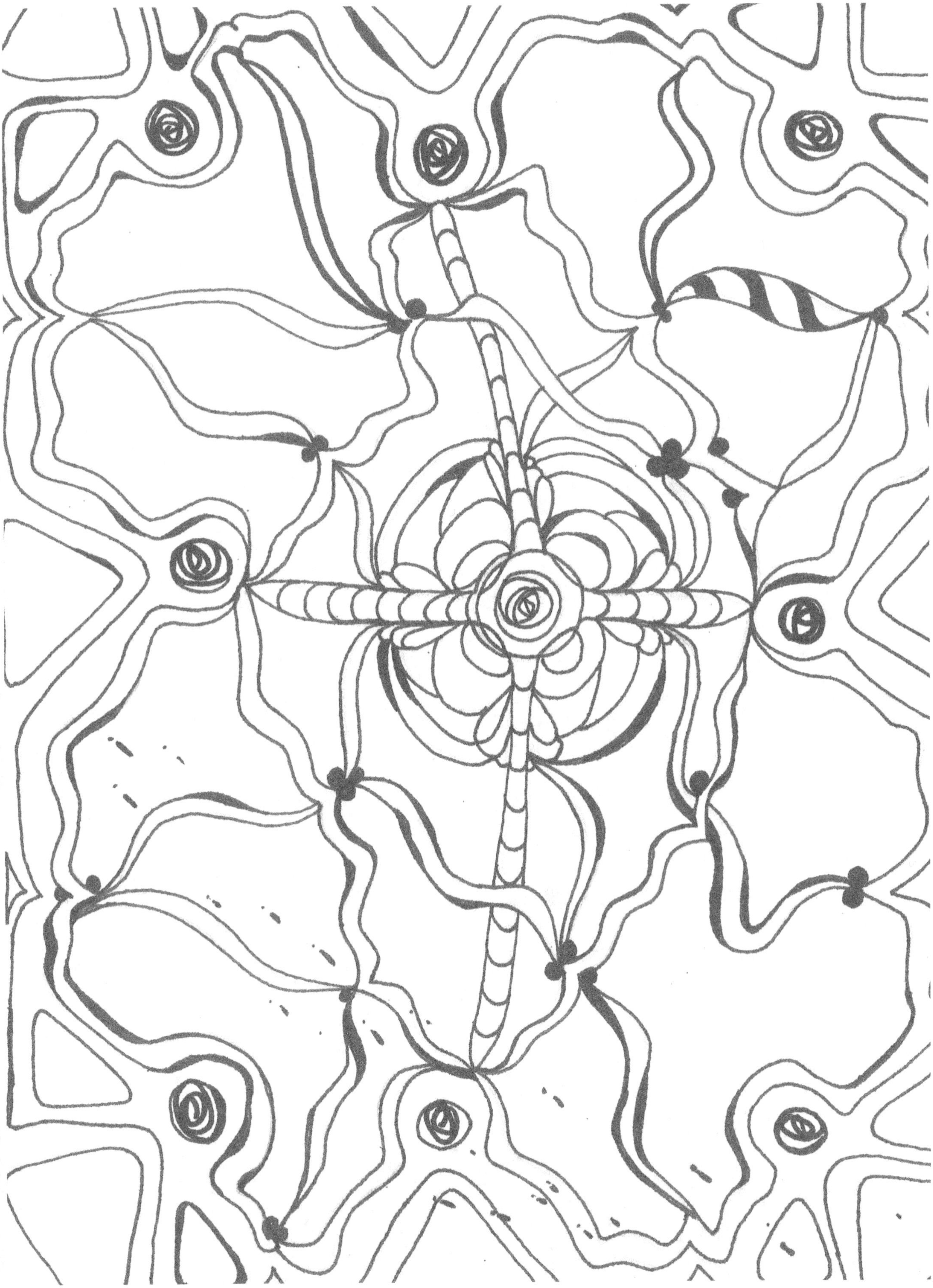

2016

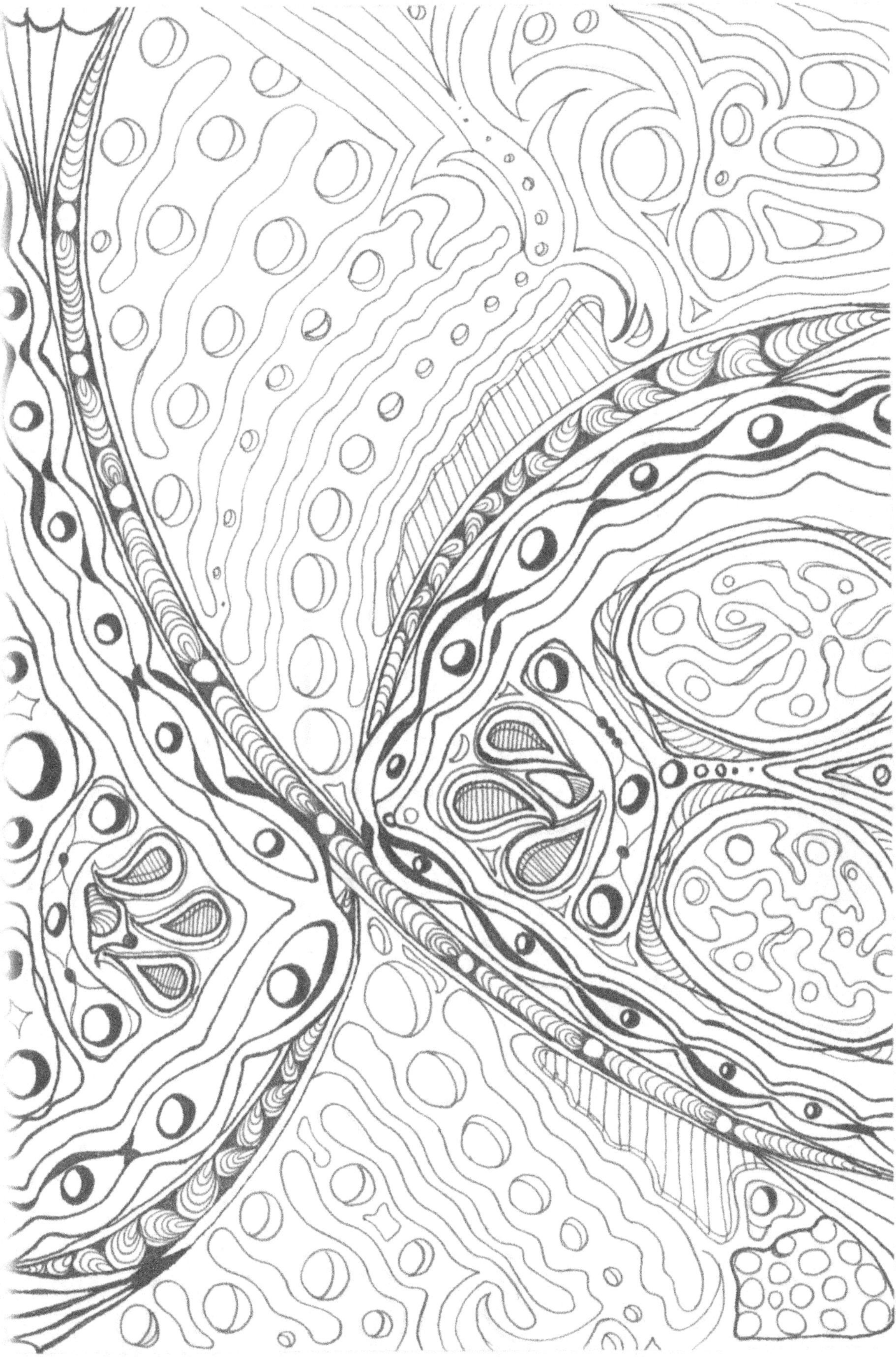

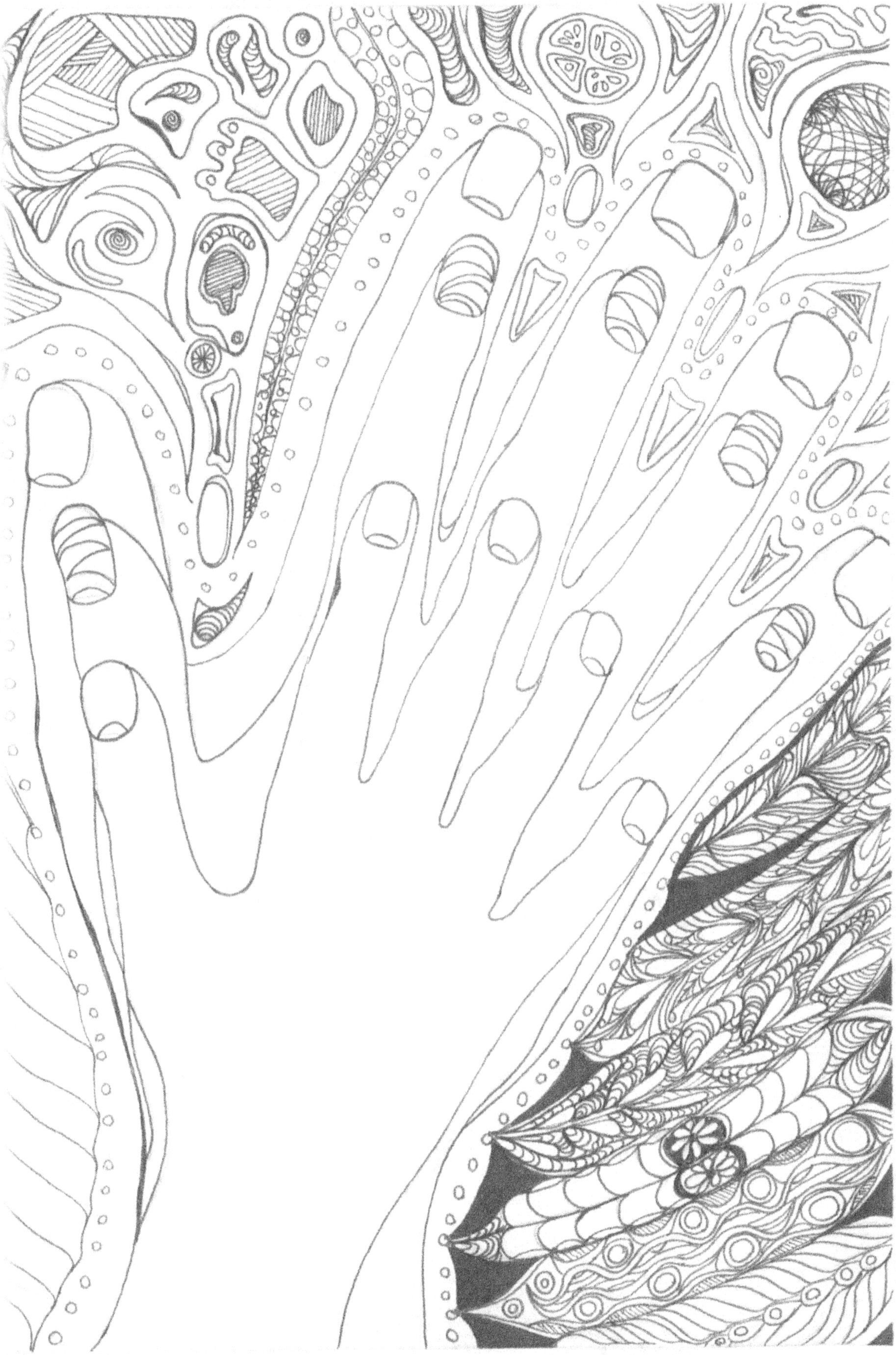

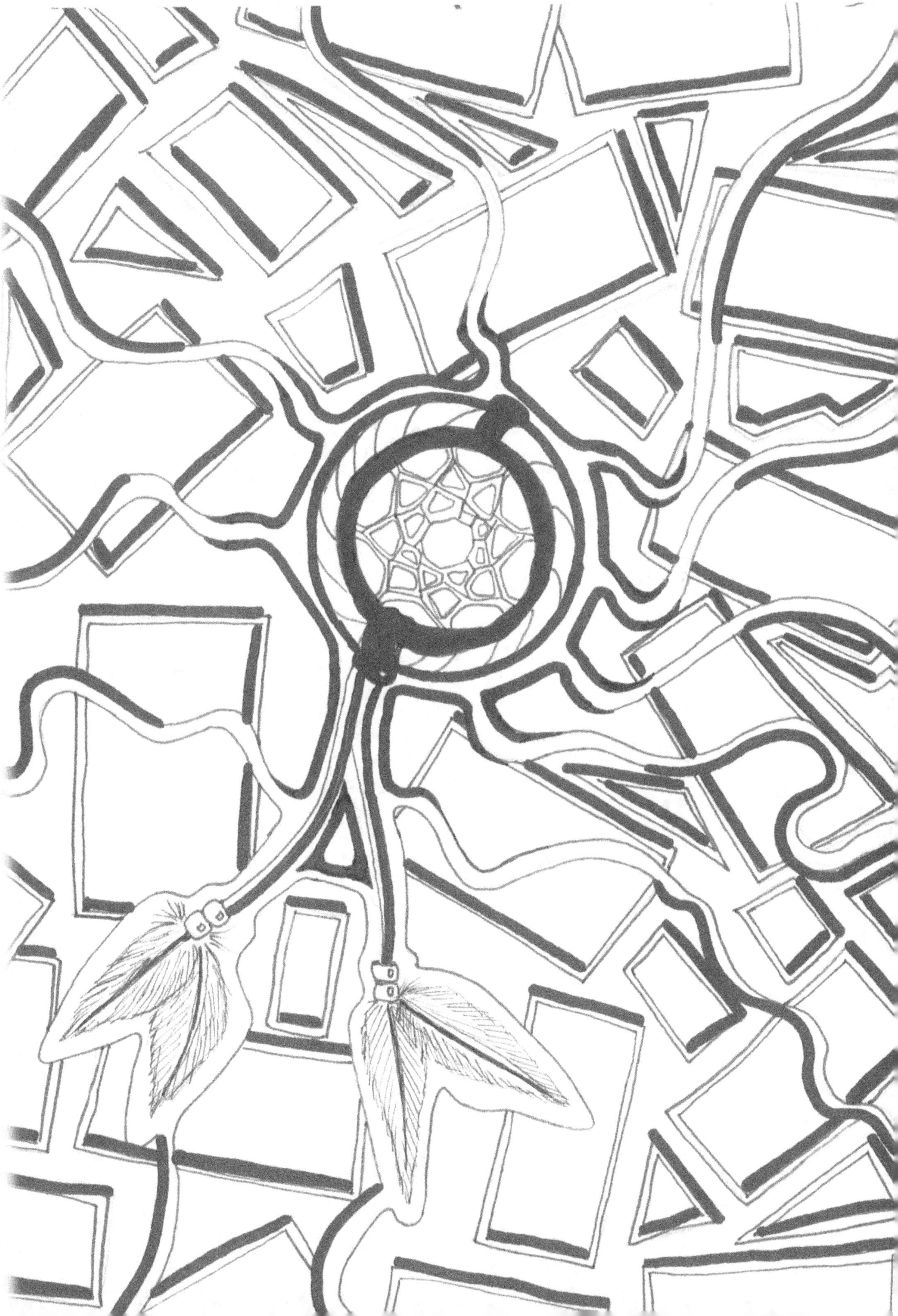

CREATE YOUR OWN.

www.ingramcontent.com/pod-product-compliance
Lightning Source LLC
Chambersburg PA
CBHW081151280526
45787CB00008B/3291
9781533341501